Copyright © 2025 by Sarah Rowan
Illustration copyright © 2025 by Sarah Rowan

All rights reserved. No portion of this book may be reproduced- mechanically, electronically, or by any other means, including photocopying - without written permission by the artist and author Sarah Rowan.

ISBN 978-1-7636150-0-7

Design by Sarah Rowan

Cover by Sarah Rowan

Written by Sarah Rowan

Proudly printed in Australia by Ingram Spark Publishing

First printing March 2025

For every soul
that forgot
they are an artist

For every artist
that has lost
a bit of their soul

For Selah & Rhema
who remind me every day
that creativity is both
a gift and a homecoming

ENDORSEMENTS

"This is such a terrific book! It reminds me of the saying 'If you say you can't you can't, but if you say you could you just might'. There is a creative soul in all of us! We just need to let it out. When I grow up I want to be an artist – I tell myself. Thank you Rowan for saying it is possible."

NAOMI SIMSON - Founder of RedBalloon & Entrepreneur

"Sarah Rowan is not just a performer; she is a visionary leader in the arts and a catalyst for positive change. Her dedication to connection, authenticity, and social impact makes her an invaluable asset to any event or organization."

ANNA SHEPPARD - Social Responsibility Expert & Top 50 Most Impactful People on LinkedIn

TABLE OF CONTENTS

INTRODUCTION	1
WHY THE CREATIVE CYCLE?	3
STEP 1 - CREATE SPACE	5
STEP 2 - USE WHAT'S IN YOUR HANDS!	11
STEP 3 - START	19
STEP 4 - HOLD YOUR IDEAS LIKE POTATO CHIPS	25
STEP 5 - STAGNATION STINKS LIKE SH*T!	32
STEP 6 - WALKABOUT	39
STEP 7 - CELEBRATE!	46
ABOUT THE AUTHOR	54
GRATITUDE (AKA ACKNOWLEDGEMENTS)	56

INTRODUCTION

What if creativity weren't reserved just for artists, but a way of living—a force that transforms the mundane into magic?

You are about to read inspirational advice from an imperfect human who loves creating art—live, in front of an audience, and under tight time constraints.

Performing for corporate audiences for over two decades has taught me a lot about what "adulting" gives and takes away—like how we trade imagination for practicality, or playfulness for productivity—when we forget we are still becoming.

One of the key ingredients to a fulfilled life is curiosity. This short and simple book is designed to support you on your journey—both personally and professionally.

Creativity is a gift within us all. When unleashed in our lives, homes, communities, and nations, problems become possibilities, challenges transform into opportunities, and fears reframe into curiosity.

Enjoy this life to the fullest. Embrace the creativity within you. And if this book sparks something in you—whether a new idea, a bold action, or a rekindled passion—share your **#TheCreativeCycle** stories with me. Let's create a movement of possibility together!

WHY THE CREATIVE CYCLE?

Starting and finishing creative projects—or any project, really—can feel daunting. In Western culture, we often view progress in a straight line: a clear beginning, middle, and end. But in many Eastern traditions, life and growth are seen through the lens of cycles. Nature itself moves in rhythms—the changing seasons, the ebb and flow of tides, the rise and fall of the sun.

If we embraced this idea, perhaps we'd be less afraid of both beginnings and endings. A project doesn't have to be perfect to be complete, just as winter doesn't apologize for giving way to spring. Every ending fertilizes the soil for something new to grow. What if, instead of fearing the unknown, we trusted in the rhythm of our own creativity—allowing it to contract and expand, pause and surge forward, just like the world around us?

Because creativity follows this same natural flow. There are times when we're in full bloom, bursting with ideas and energy, like spring. And there are times when we need to retreat, rest, and reflect—our creative winter. The struggle comes when we resist these cycles, expecting constant productivity when our minds and bodies are calling for renewal. Or when we sit idly, binge-watching an entire series, during what should be a season of planting seeds for future growth.

Understanding the cycle of creativity helps us work with it rather than against it. Successful creatives recognize their own rhythm, name their own steps, and learn to navigate the flow. After two decades of performing as a live painter, I've identified the steps that shape my creative cycle. They may evolve over time, but for now—this is how I roll. My hope is that these insights become an asset to your life, your relationships, and your work.

STEP 1

**Physically.
Emotionally.
Spiritually.**

Creativity thrives in space. Not just physical space, but emotional, mental, and even spiritual space. If your mind, schedule, and heart are cluttered, there's little room for new ideas to take root, let alone flourish.

Think of creativity like a breath—it needs room to expand. When we're constantly consumed with to-do lists, obligations, and noise (both external and internal), our ability to think innovatively is suffocated. Without space, ideas don't have the oxygen to ignite.

Creating space doesn't require a fancy studio, a week-long retreat, or a total life overhaul. It can be as simple as lying in the grass, closing your eyes, and letting your mind wander without expectation. It's in these unscripted, unforced moments that creativity sneaks in—offering solutions to work dilemmas, clarity on relationships, or reviving long-buried dreams.

Making space can look different for everyone. Maybe it's decluttering a corner of your home and claiming it as your creative nook. Maybe it's scheduling 10 minutes of silence before jumping into your daily routine. Maybe it's a mindful walk, a deep breath between tasks, or even saying no to something that drains your energy.

Sometimes, making space means physically changing your environment. Studies have shown that rearranging your workspace, shifting furniture, or even altering the lighting in your creative area can stimulate new neural pathways, sparking fresh ideas and enhancing problem-solving skills. Small changes in your surroundings can lead to major shifts in how your brain approaches creativity.

Space isn't just for you—it's also about the people around you. Collaboration flourishes in environments where creativity has room to stretch. When you allow yourself the freedom to create, you inspire others to do the same.

So, where can you carve out space today? Physically, emotionally, spiritually—start small, and watch what unfolds.

Physically:
Create or clean your creative space. Rearrange the furniture! Natural light and indoor plants are bonuses

Emotionally:
Let go of fear and your inner critic by telling them they can have the day off

Spiritually:
Still your restless mind with meditation, singing, dancing, gardening, etc.

STEP 2

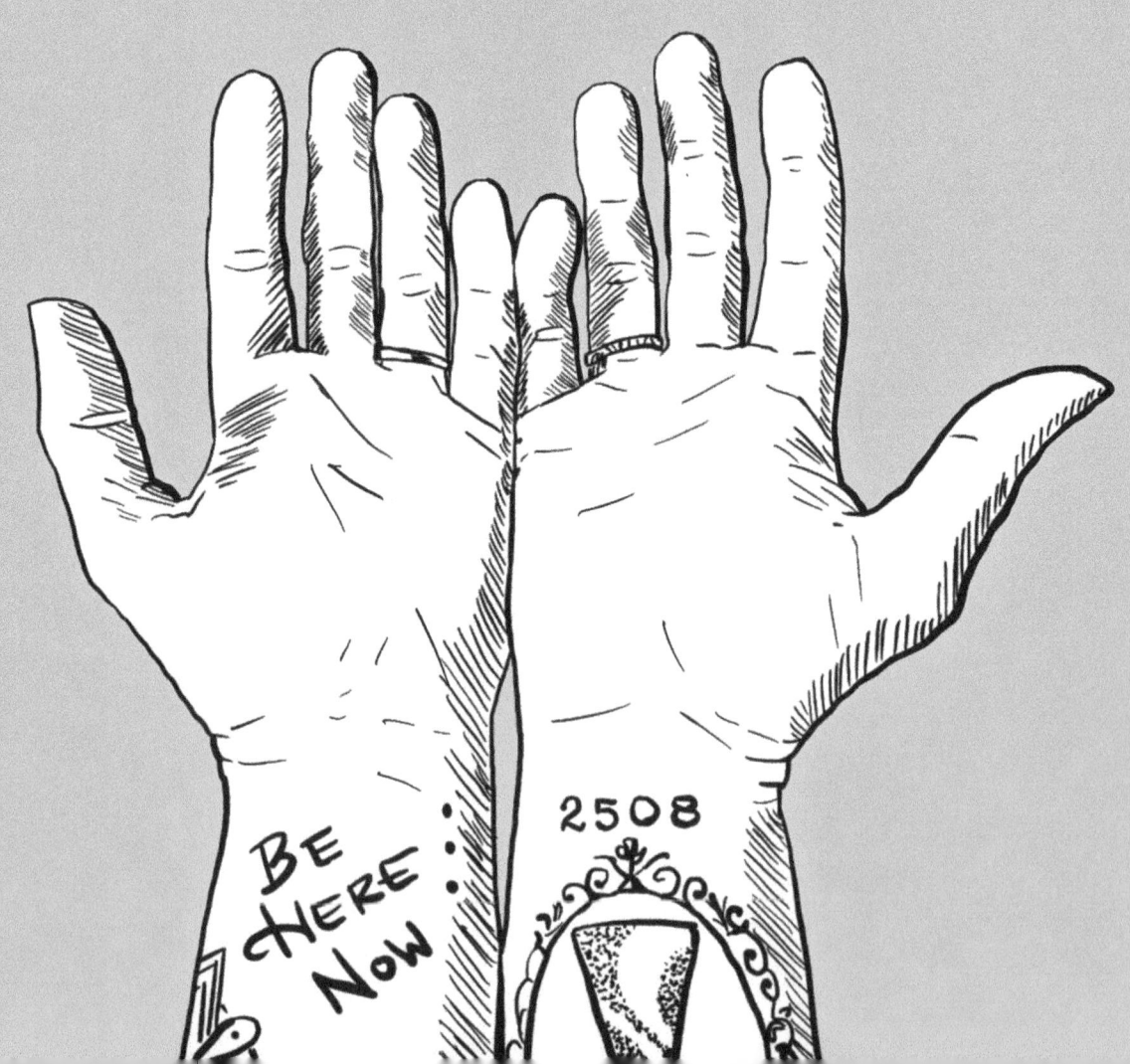

"Ditch the comparison game. You are enough. And you have nothing to prove."

SARAH ROWAN

You have talents within you that you haven't even begun to unlock. Creativity isn't reserved for the "gifted" or those with artistic careers—it's woven into how we solve problems, connect ideas, and navigate life itself. And guess what? You already have the essential ingredients to create something extraordinary.

Too often, we believe creativity requires something outside of us—a bigger budget, more time, fancier tools, or even permission from someone else. But the truth is, the most powerful resources you will ever need are already in your hands. Creativity is less about what you have and more about how you use it.

Imagine a sculptor staring at a block of marble. The masterpiece isn't something they find elsewhere—it's something they uncover by working with what's right in front of them. You, too, have raw materials waiting to be shaped. Maybe you've already noticed them. Maybe they've been lying dormant. Either way, they are there.

Creativity isn't just about artistic skill—it's a mindset. A way of approaching life. Whether you consider yourself "creative" or not, you already have at least one of these powerful ingredients:

CURIOSITY – Do you ask questions? Wonder how things work? Challenge the status quo? Curiosity is the spark that fuels discovery. In fact, it's considered one of the most important—if not the most essential—traits to cultivate as AI continues to transform every industry. Nurture the seed of curiosity within you, and it will not disappoint!

OPEN-MINDEDNESS – Do you embrace new perspectives, ideas, and experiences? Creativity thrives where rigidity dies. The more open you are, the more possibilities will reveal themselves—often in the most unexpected places.

IMAGINATION – Can you see possibilities beyond what currently exists? Every innovation, story, and breakthrough began with someone imagining "what if?" Personally, I love a good daydream—and I'm convinced the world would be brighter if we all hit pause on the serious stuff now and then and let our minds play a little.

FLEXIBILITY – Can you pivot when things don't go as planned? Creative thinkers adapt, experiment, and find solutions in unexpected places.

PERSISTANCE – Are you willing to push through failure, doubt, and roadblocks? Creativity isn't about perfection—it's about showing up again and again.

PASSION – Do you have something that excites or energizes you? Passion is the fuel that turns ideas into action. It's the heartbeat of creativity—without it, even the best ideas struggle to come alive.

RISK-TAKING – Are you willing to try, even when success isn't guaranteed? Innovation comes from those brave enough to step into the unknown.

COLLABORATION – Do you bounce ideas off others, seek feedback, and co-create? The best ideas often emerge from shared energy and perspectives.

PLAYFULNESS – Can you explore without pressure, make mistakes, and enjoy the process? Play invites experimentation and breaks down creative fear.

ABILITY TO REFLECT – Do you take time to process, refine, and learn from experiences? Reflection deepens understanding and helps creativity evolve.

Taking inspiration from the list of creative "Ingredients," choose one each day this week to play with in your everyday life.

How would a curious outsider approach the challenges you are currently facing? How would a child with an unshackled imagination look for solutions to your problems? Sometimes, when we remove our fears and emotions from a situation and observe it like a stranger, it becomes far easier to find resolutions.

Lastly, **do something for someone else.**

Solve their problem. Is your elderly neighbour lonely? Invite them over for dinner. I believe the biggest acts of creativity are simply acts of love and generosity.

STEP 3

"Daydreaming doesn't make art. Making art makes art."

SARAH ROWAN

If I had a completed painting for every daydream I had about a painting, I could fill every major gallery in every major city. Not that 10% of my daydream artworks are worthy of display, but you get my drift, yeah?

Starting is often one of the hardest parts of any project, major life decisions, or creative endeavour. Blank canvases are intimidating! Some days they have minds and voices of their own—whispering or shouting every limiting belief they can until you put it aside for another day.

To silence my inner critic and start any project, I just grab whatever colour or colours I feel like at that moment and cover the canvas as quickly as possible. Sometimes, by the end of the painting, you can no longer see my initial colour, but who cares?! Once you begin moving, it is a lot easier to keep going!

Momentum has begun, and a state of flow is closer than before...

What does starting look like for you?

Does it resemble buying a pair of runners to exercise during your lunch hour, or finally tuning your piano so you can sit down and play it? Perhaps it's enrolling in night school to acquire the credentials needed for your dream job. Maybe it's simply picking up the brush, writing the first line, or saying yes to an opportunity before you feel fully ready.

TIP: When you focus on the journey of creating—rather than clinging to a perfect "fairy tale ending"—you'll enjoy the process more and be more likely to finish what you start.

Action fuels momentum, and momentum fuels creativity.

Sometimes, starting looks like finishing.

Is it time to end a toxic relationship to pave the way for a life of fulfilment? Or perhaps it's breaking free from cycles of self-sabotage with the support of friends, a therapist, or through mindfulness practices? It could even mean letting go of an outdated identity—one that no longer serves who you are becoming. Starting isn't always about adding more to your life; sometimes, it's about making space by clearing away what no longer fits.

In life, we often need to close significant chapters before we can embark on new beginnings. Because every great story has turning points, and sometimes, the bravest thing you can do is write The End before daring to begin again.

(Stay tuned… this is a running theme for my next book…)

STEP 4

"Hold your ideas like potato chips.

Too tightly and you'll crush creativity. Too loosely and they will fall from your hand.

Just right and you can munch your way to innovation."

SARAH ROWAN

During my high school cross-country days, my coach would often remind me to hold my hands as if they contained delicate potato chips. She would say, "if you hold your hands tightly you will reduce the flow of oxygen throughout your body, and if you hold them too loosely, you will waste unnecessary energy as they flop around."

At the time, I thought it was just a quirky coaching tip. But years later, I realized how this simple mental image applies to so much more than running—it's a perfect metaphor for how we hold onto ideas.

How often have you experienced a surge of inspiration, only to suffocate it with overthinking, over-talking, and over-analyzing? You grip the idea so tightly, trying to mold it into something perfect before it even has room to breathe. And just like crushing a fragile chip in a clenched fist, you squeeze the life out of your own creativity.

Great ideas need intentional space.

Think about it—when you hold a potato chip gently, it stays intact, ready to be enjoyed. But if you grip it too hard? Crumbs. The same goes for creativity. The best ideas often arrive like whispers, delicate and fleeting. If you try to control them too forcefully, they crumble under pressure.

So, next time inspiration strikes, resist the urge to strangle it with logic or drown it in endless planning. Instead, hold it lightly. Let it breathe. Give it the space to evolve naturally.

Some of the greatest ideas in history started as nothing more than a passing thought—handled with care, nurtured with curiosity, and given just enough room to grow.

And let's be real—potato chips are best enjoyed when they're whole. So, treat your ideas the same way.

TAKE ACTION

When the muse whispers in your ear (or shouts at you in the shower), jot it down. Capture it before it drifts away, but resist the urge to immediately parade it around like a trophy. Some ideas need quiet incubation before they face the world.

Avoid over-sharing—not just to prevent someone from "borrowing" your brilliance, but because talking about an idea too much can trick your brain into thinking you've already done something with it. Like adding water to concentrated juice, endless discussion dilutes the essence of what made it exciting in the first place.

Instead, choose wisely who you let in. Once you've thoughtfully shared your idea, embrace feedback. Even if you believe your concept is flawless—or totally dismissible—reconsider.

Some of the worst ideas in history were pitched with absolute confidence—think the baby mop, Smell-O-Vision, and spray-on hair. Meanwhile, some of the greatest ideas ever invented—the automobile, airplane, and telephone—were met with deep skepticism before they changed the world.

Not every idea is a golden, crispy masterpiece. Some need refining, some need reshaping, and some are best discarded like burnt potato chips. The key is knowing the difference.

Seek out a trusted friend or colleague—someone who will challenge you, not just cheerlead you. Candid, constructive insight is like taste-testing before launching a new flavour. You wouldn't serve an entire bag of chips without making sure they're edible first.

Most importantly—makers gotta make. Ideas are only as good as the action that follows. So, hold them gently, move them forward, and when it's time—crunch in.

STEP 5

"Let creativity flow like wet paint.

Keep it moving, morphing, breathing.

It will come alive if you let it."

SARAH ROWAN

During my university days, my painting professor shared invaluable advice. She warned against spending the entire 3-hour class fixated on one aspect of the canvas, explaining that it would hinder reaching a state of flow in subsequent sessions.

Instead of growing stagnant in one spot, she encouraged a steady, almost cyclical approach, ensuring each part of the canvas received attention, leading to a more cohesive work in the long term.

The same principle applies to life. Have you ever found yourself pouring all your energy into one area, only to watch other parts unravel? Consider the classic workaholic who neglects family relationships due to their relentless focus on career, or the health enthusiast so obsessed with diet that they forget the importance of movement.

Creativity, like water, needs movement. A flowing river stays clear and full of life, while stagnant water breeds decay, murkiness, and mosquitoes. The same goes for the creative mind—if you fixate too long in one spot, ideas stop moving, inspiration turns stale, and frustration creeps in.

If you're feeling stuck, step back. Shift your focus. Work on another part of the canvas—whether that canvas is your art, your career, your health, or your personal life. Inspiration thrives in circulation.

Stagnant water stinks, attracts pests, and eventually dries up. Don't let it bite you on the bum—keep moving, keep creating, and let your life flow.

Take some time over the following week to observe how you spend your time, money, and energy in every area of your life.

Be honest with yourself: Is it working? Are you creating a masterpiece, or are certain areas feeling overworked, neglected, or muddied?

Consider how you can paint your life to bring more flow to your experiences. Reflect on what needs attention—what needs to be painted over, what craves a bright splash of colour, and where could use some fine line work? What details have you been overlooking that could bring everything into balance?

Remember that life is one big canvas. If you need a fresh start, grab a big brush and base coat it anew. Embrace the opportunity for renewal and transformation. Don't be afraid to experiment—some of the most breathtaking art emerges from unexpected strokes.

Shift your perspective from asking, "Why does [X] keep happening to me?" to asking, "What is this teaching me?"

Be prepared for some wild style changes to your life canvas when you start asking that question—it has the power to shift the entire narrative. And the best part? You are both the artist and the artwork in progress.

STEP 6

"We are just visitors to this time, this place. We are just passing through.

Our purpose here is to observe, to learn, to grow and to love...and then we return home."

AUSTRALIAN ABORIGINAL PROVERB

When you're deep in a project, it's easy to lose perspective. Staring at the same thing for too long can make even the best ideas feel dull. That's why one of the most powerful creative tools isn't pushing harder—it's stepping away.

In Indigenous Australian culture, Walkabout is a deeply spiritual journey, a sacred coming-of-age ceremony for young Aboriginal boys between the ages of 10-16. A time of true connection to Country, self, and tradition. While not everyone experiences it in this way, the idea of taking space to gain clarity is universal. Sometimes, the best way to find fresh inspiration is to physically remove yourself—take a walk, switch environments, or do something completely unrelated.

Your brain and soul does incredible work in the background when you give it room to breathe. So, the next time you feel stuck, don't force it—step away, reset, and return with fresh eyes. You'll be surprised what you see.

Sometimes when I'm painting on large canvases, it's challenging to see the full picture until I step back and view it from a distance. Life too, presents a similar challenge. Amidst the busyness of our lives, it's difficult to discern what needs attention, fixing, tender loving care, or even painting over.

When I'm refining a keynote, I imagine myself in the audience—curious, open, and observing. I mentally step outside myself and just listen. After a few minutes of disconnecting from the performer in me, I begin to hear the deeper wisdom rising from my subconscious. That's often where the gold is hiding.

As humans, we can find ourselves lost and drifting through life, feeling out of control. In such moments, when our vision becomes clouded and our connection to self wanes, I believe **it's crucial to step away from the routines of daily life and surrender to the journey back to ourselves.**

TAKE ACTION

Step away from the projects, stress, and conversations that have consumed your life. Give your mind space to breathe. Take a walk in nature—leave your tech behind—and fully immerse yourself in the beauty around you.

Practice mindfulness by focusing on your breath. Observe your thoughts without judgment, as if you were a casual visitor passing through your own mind. Buddhist monks often refer to the restless, scattered mind as the "monkey mind"—always chattering, jumping from thought to thought. The key isn't to silence it but to gently guide it, using deep, intentional breaths to anchor yourself in the present.

Kick off your shoes and connect with the earth—whether it's sand, grass, or stone—wherever you are, let yourself be present. Sand, in particular, carries negatively charged ions, which can help neutralize stress in the body, restore balance, and boost overall well-being.

Reflect on who you are and the person you aspire to be. How would they think, speak, act, dress, work, and engage with the world around them? How do they treat others? How do they treat themselves?

Now, identify small, intentional changes you can make each day to align more closely with this vision of your best self.

(If movement is a challenge for you, explore new ways to shift your environment—whether through music, scent, or a guided journey with a friend. A fresh perspective is always within reach.)

STEP 7

"Embrace what makes you different. Own your quirks.

Back yourself—because if you don't, who will?"

SARAH ROWAN

Do you take the time to truly celebrate your wins?

So often, we achieve something—a work milestone, a personal goal, even just making it through a tough season—only to move straight onto the next challenge without stopping to acknowledge it. In today's fast-paced world, we're constantly ticking things off a never-ending to-do list, rarely pausing to reflect on how far we've come. But life deserves to be celebrated, not just in big moments, but in the small, meaningful ways that bring us joy.

For me, celebrations don't have to be grand. A simple dinner with family, an ocean swim, planting new seedlings in my garden, or even getting a tattoo—these are the rituals that help me mark the moments that matter. They are a reminder to pause, reflect, and appreciate the journey.

How do you celebrate yourself? Your relationships? The moments that make life special?

TAKE ACTION

Pause for a moment. Close your eyes and take a deep breath. Now, think back to a version of yourself from five years ago. What would they say if they could see you now?

Chances are, they'd be proud. Surprised. Maybe even a little in awe. Because no matter how chaotic life feels, you have grown. You have achieved things. But do you actually take the time to celebrate that?

In today's world, we rush from one thing to the next, barely stopping to acknowledge our own progress. If you never celebrate yourself, you're training your brain to believe that nothing is ever "enough." And that's a trap.

So here's your challenge:

Once a month, mark your progress on purpose. It doesn't have to be grand. Maybe it's a sunrise swim. A journal entry. A slow, mindful cup of coffee with no distractions. A playlist of songs that remind you how far you've come.

Make it a ritual. Make it yours. And while you're at it—celebrate the people you love, too. Because gratitude grows exponentially when we share it.

You are not the same person you were a year ago, a month ago, or even last week. Every step forward, no matter how small, is proof that you are moving, learning, and evolving.

So don't just let life blur past—claim your moments, own your journey, and celebrate the masterpiece that is you!

What will your celebration look like this month?

ABOUT THE AUTHOR

Sarah Rowan is an award-winning artist and international keynote speaker who empowers individuals and organisations to ignite a better future through creativity.

As one of Australia's top, speed painters, she has lived and breathed the dynamic process of transformation for over 20 years, turning blank walls and canvasses into thought-provoking pieces of art, with limited time and often in front of a live audience. Merging her artistic talent with her passion for public speaking, Rowan has reimagined the role of the artist, pushing the boundaries of a studio-based pursuit into a trail-blazing performance genre that challenges the limitations of time and space.

She lives in Sydney, Australia and online at
www.artistsarahrowan.com

©2025 by Sarah Rowan   artistsarahrowan@gmail.com

ACCESS MY WEBSITE, SOCIALS, AND LEAVE A REVIEW!
BUT MORE IMPORTANTLY—I'D LOVE TO HEAR YOUR STORY!
HOW HAS THE CREATIVITY CYCLE SPARKED NEW IDEAS IN YOUR LIFE?

SHARE YOUR JOURNEY WITH ME ON SOCIAL MEDIA AND TAG ME —I MIGHT JUST FEATURE YOUR STORY!

GRATITUDE

Look, I know—it's a short book, but don't be fooled! This little book took years of procrastination, overthinking, and life crises to finally make it into your hands. So yes, a thank-you page is absolutely necessary.

Mum & Dad – I wouldn't exist without you (literally), and I'm forever grateful you encouraged my wild artistic dreams instead of steering me toward a "real job".

My lover…Lizzie – You are my greatest muse and the keeper of all my weird, wonderful potato-chip ideas. Because of you, creativity feels effortless.

Selah & Rhema – For cheering on a mother whose career choices are as bizarre as her personality. Your love and support means the world to me.

The Kalie Kids - Being your step "mom" is absolutely wild and I've learned that step-parenting is kind of like abstract art—confusing, unpredictable, and strangely beautiful!

Clarissa Fe Reyes – Your layout and tech wizardry transformed my scattered ideas into something beautiful. You took my vanilla tech skills and added the whipped cream and sprinkles!

Michael Arnot & Marty Wilson – A massive thank you for your coaching, wisdom, and for making sure I actually finished this book instead of adding it to my "one day" list. Thank you for helping me push through 100 title ideas!

And finally—to **you, dear reader**—for picking up this book, flipping through these pages, and letting me be a small part of your creative journey. May you take what's inside, run with it, and create something that fills you with wonder.

With a heart full of gratitude and hands covered in paint...